When Will I
Stop Hurting?

When Will I Stop Hurting?

Dealing with a Recent Death

June Cerza Kolf

Baker Books

A Division of Baker Book House Co
Grand Rapids, Michigan 49516

© 1987, 2001 by June Cerza Kolf

Published by Baker Books
a division of Baker Book House Company
P.O. Box 6287, Grand Rapids, MI 49516-6287

Fifth printing, November 2005

Printed in the United States of America

Library of Congress Cataloging-in-Publication Data is on file at the Library of Congress, Washington, D.C.

ISBN 0-8010-6385-X

Scripture quotations are from *The Living Bible,* © 1971. Used by permission of Tyndale House Publishers, Inc., Wheaton, IL 60189. All rights reserved.

All the names have been changed and situations have been disguised so as to not inflict any pain on my friends, family, business associates, or the bereavement group.

To my daughters,
their husbands,
and my grandchildren,
whose unconditional love,
patience, support, practical assistance, compassion,
and understanding have been endless.

Contents

Preface

When I originally wrote this book, my children were almost raised, and I had prayed for a useful way to spend my time. My hospice work came about as the result of a string of unusual circumstances, and I knew it had to be none other than God's choice for me to pursue it. I found the work rewarding and fulfilling. The bereavement portion of my job came so naturally that I began to concentrate more time and effort in that area, and it resulted in this book and several others.

At the time I began my work, all my family members were alive and healthy. However, during the first year at my job, I lost three close relatives and my best friend. I was suddenly surrounded with intense losses, both at home and at work. It continued that way for several years.

I "retired" from my career when my husband retired from his thirty-plus years at NASA. We spent the next few years primarily traveling around the U.S. or planning the next trip. Four years into our retirement, our journey took a dramatic turn. My husband was diagnosed with bladder cancer, and we began our personal battle against that deadly disease. A year and a half later, after intensive treatment and hospice care, he lost his courageous fight, and I found myself on the path where I had led so many others for all those years.

The question I am asked most frequently is, "What would you change in your book now that you've personally experienced the death of your husband?" In all honesty, I have to admit there is nothing I would change. At the time I wrote *When Will I Stop Hurting?*, I said it was God's book, and I was simply the typist. That fact holds true today. I have reread this book many times since my own loss and use it as my own handbook.

Contrary to what many people have expressed to me, I am not a "grief expert," and it has been no easier for me than anyone else. Because I have the information memorized and can present workshops or feel completely comfortable at funerals does not mean that my heart is any less bruised or battered. Each day is a challenge for all grievers, whether they have spent their career working in the field of death and dying or whether they are experiencing their first brush with death.

I lean heavily on the Lord for strength. I shed abundant tears and call upon my friends and family frequently as I search daily for answers and comfort. Over the years I have watched hundreds of people find their way to new, meaningful lives after the death of a loved one, so I am never without hope.

I am now "walking the walk" as I watch the horizon for my very own rainbow.

Acknowledgments

A special thank you to:

The many people who opened the doors of their grief and allowed me to peek inside,

My friends, who supported me during Jack's illness and the year that followed,

And to God, who chose me to be the typist for his book.

ONE

The Wound

In working with grieving persons, I have become aware that there is a great need for grief to be understood. This book is not meant to give instructions or advice. Instead it is a series of quotes, suggestions, affirmations, and explanations intended to console, to reassure, and especially to offer hope to anyone who is suffering from the agonizing loss of a loved one. Although every person grieves in an individual way, there are some common denominators. It is my hope to bring comfort to grieving persons by letting them know they are not alone in their experiences or feelings.

The death of a loved one is a mortal wound, difficult to grasp and impossible to understand. It is unasked for, unplanned for, and unwanted. It is one of the few events in life that is beyond human control. Because of the depth of the wound, even one's own self becomes unfamiliar. Time assumes a different meaning, and nothing that was once important matters any longer. One woman told me, "It may be six months since the death of my child, but to me it has been one long, ghastly day with no beginning and no end."

The "ghastly days" must somehow be survived, often with little help and no past frame of reference. Grief seems to be a process that cannot be understood or explained unless one has personally experienced it.

Fay Angus in *How to Do Everything Right and Live to Regret It* says she had not reckoned on the sting of hurt that peels away the layers like leaves on an artichoke, being nibbled one by one until all that is exposed is the heart.[1]

Having our hearts exposed is an extremely vulnerable position to be in. It can make us feel persecuted and alone. *Why did this happen to me?* we ask.

It happened partly because we were fortunate enough to have loved someone. Without love there would be no grief. So we need to ask ourselves instead, *Would I be willing to exchange my disabling grief for never having known my lost loved one? Are the love and the happy memories we shared worth my current pain? If I had known I would eventually suffer this loss, would I have turned away from the love to avoid the pain?*

When a loss occurs to people who believe in God, we often ask for the reason he allowed such a horrendous thing to happen. If we pray for the healing of a loved one and it does not occur, we feel God has forsaken us. *Where was God when I needed him most?* we cry.

God never promised us a utopia on earth or a life free from pain. J. Grant Swank, Jr., says,

> Good folk and innocent people are not without their share of suffering—and often through no fault of their own. They are not immune to hard times. Indeed, believers can experience pain just as severely as nonbelievers. Being a child of God does not exempt one from anguish or from the heaviness of sorrow that bends the heart near the point of breaking.[2]

What God does promise is that he will never leave us during our times of trouble (Ps. 34:19).

I once heard about an elderly couple who had been married many years. The husband was driving along the highway when his wife spotted a young couple sitting very close

14

together in the next car. She wistfully said to her husband, "Remember when we used to be like that?"

Her husband smiled at her and gently said, "Honey, I haven't moved."

Although we may feel farther from God in times of great need or sorrow, he is never the one who moves away. He never leaves the driver's seat. He simply sits there, patiently waiting for us to move closer.

Grief is a heavy burden that can seem backbreaking, but a heavy load of any type will seem lighter when it is shared with a friend. I believe God has very large, strong shoulders. He will gladly help carry our load of grief if only we are willing to not clutch it so tightly.

The Symptoms of Grief

In the process of holding tightly to our grief we may become forgetful and unable to make decisions. If we were previously quite organized we may suddenly become completely disorganized. We can get lost driving home from the neighborhood store where we have shopped for years. We might forget the ends of sentences or be unable to remember words or names. We do not care how we look, how we feel, or what we do. We feel sad, isolated, and alone.

We find ourselves crying over everything. When we least expect it, tears fill our eyes and make trails down our cheeks. We become afraid to go places or see people for fear these unpredictable tears will begin to flow again. We also cry as we never have before; our deep, wretched sobbing comes from the bottom of a black chasm that we never imagined existed.

In general the whole world seems to be turned upside down. A soft-spoken person might suddenly find himself shouting at his children. Or an extrovert may become fearful of attending a meeting. We are pulled in opposite directions. We are agitated but too tired to move; we are lonely but don't want to be with others; we feel unloved, unloving, and unlovable, yet we need love desperately. We feel as if we have been abandoned and as if our nerve endings are raw.

Physical symptoms may hit without warning—hot flashes, cold sweats, insomnia, loss of appetite, tightness in the chest, rapid breathing—and can be very distressing. A complete medical checkup can eliminate the possibility of these symptoms being caused by a legitimate ailment.

Many grieving persons ignore danger signs, assuming that the discomfort is merely part of their grief, and often their lack of energy prevents them from seeking medical care. Some minor ailments can become debilitating if they go untreated too long. With a proper diagnosis it may be possible to begin to feel physically stronger and thus make it easier to cope emotionally.

The survivor who has been involved in caring for a loved one during a lengthy terminal illness may have neglected self-care during that time. Dental and eye examinations may be needed in addition to a thorough physical.

Then a horrendous fear that cannot be identified sets in: *I feel as if I am going crazy.* This fear never seems to go away, and there is no way to reason with it while it nags and hovers; it may ease up a bit, but it never completely disappears.

These symptoms are all the unexplained, untalked about, misunderstood feelings of profound grief.

Feelings of Guilt

Guilt is another unwelcome guest to the grieving. It creeps around the corners of our minds, especially in the middle of the night when we cannot sleep. *Why didn't I make John go*

*to the doctor sooner? I should have made Bill stop smoking.
I should have driven Susan to school that day.*

Phrases that begin with *Why didn't I* and *I should have* are never constructive. Although it is necessary to think everything through and go over the details after the death of a loved one before coming to any kind of acceptance, if the thoughts become mainly ones of guilt it may be time to apply "thought stopping" or "interruption."

This technique is done by using the command *Stop!*, then rethinking the situation using affirmations, such as *It's a good thing I did not nag Bill about smoking. It would have made him miserable.*

The past cannot be changed; it can only be accepted. With an acceptance of the past comes the possibility to plan the future. Torturing ourselves for things that can no longer be altered takes tremendous energy. A grieving person already has a low energy level, so it is foolish to waste the short supply. We must treat ourselves gently to allow the memories to heal.

Forgiveness

Forgiveness is not a very big word. It is not difficult to pronounce or spell, but it can take control of our entire lives. Jesus spoke of forgiveness just prior to his death when he asked God to forgive the people who had crucified him.

I often speak with people who have had a loved one taken from them as the result of a drunk driver. They are seething with rage. Frequently the driver walks away from the accident unscathed. I cannot ask someone to forgive an assailant of this sort. Only with the grace of God and the support of family, therapy groups, and friends would it be thinkable.

However, unforgiveness will stand in the way of the normal healing of a severely wounded soul. Similar to a wound that is closed with the putrid infection inside, a wounded soul will continue to fester underneath until eventually it will spew hatred, anger, resentment, bitterness, and vengefulness into every inch of a being. It will allow no room for goodness, joy, kindness, or love to flow through.

Unforgiveness can destroy the rest of our lives and the lives of everyone we touch. Holding a grudge hurts the bearer more than the recipient.

I have no pat answers for an unforgiving heart, but I do see the damage that can be done by cold, hard hearts. Each person must evaluate his or her specific situation and discover an appropriate solution, weighing the damage that will be done as hatred eats at the soul versus the doors that will be opened after forgiveness takes place.

Not long ago I had contact with two widows and their stepchildren; their contrasting actions reinforced this theory. One widow angrily told me she would not give one single item that had belonged to her husband to his sons. "They aren't *my* sons; they don't deserve a thing. I don't even plan to see them again," she said, her eyes flashing with hatred as she nursed ancient hurts.

The other widow, Ann, arrived one evening at our meeting with a big smile on her face. When asked about her unexpected happiness, she explained that the night before she had invited her two stepsons over for dinner. They had never been close, and she was not even sure they would come. Ann was pleased when they did. After dinner she provided each boy with a large empty box.

"I want you to have whatever you want of your father's," she told them. They walked through the house together while Ann opened desk drawers, closets, and even used a flashlight as they toured the backyard. The boys were hesitant at first, but she kept reassuring them she was serious.

Ann admitted that she did falter as one boy lifted his dad's Western belt off the closet hook. The large silver buckle was worn smooth from years of wear. She said her heart gave a lurch and her face flushed with heat. But she forced herself to smile and nod her approval as she swallowed hard.

She told us she was pleased with her decisions. She thought about how happy this sharing would have made her husband. If she had selfishly hoarded the belt, it would have been sealed in a box and placed in storage.

The other widow will never experience the peace of mind that Ann will. Her attitude will only harm herself as it festers inside.

Forgiving ourselves is just as important as forgiving others. Guilt is a form of unforgiveness for our mistakes or omissions. To continue to agonize over matters we can no longer change is self-defeating. We can learn from those mistakes and not repeat them. Only then can we move forward, forgiving ourselves and others. When we no longer harbor hatred, seek revenge, or bear grudges, we no longer sap our energy and prevent progress.

The Duration of Grief

Naturally, when we are feeling such torment we want to know when we will begin to feel better. We become quite accustomed to doing things according to schedule. We are told to allow six weeks to recover from gallbladder surgery and that it takes two hours to drive to the city.

In my work with the grieving the question I am most frequently asked is, "When will I stop hurting so much?" I wish there were a chart I could turn to for an answer. But even if there were such a chart it would be meaningless, because time now has an entirely new meaning.

A day is no longer a twenty-four-hour period. It is instead minute after minute filled with pain. There are no pills, no beverages, no magic formulas for the suffering. Trying to ease the pain with alcohol or drugs will only delay the normal grief process.

Recovering from the death of a loved one has been termed "grief work" by the experts. It is indeed work, work that takes time. Like any other job, it cannot be rushed, nor can it be gauged by anyone else's progress. Too many factors have to be calculated, too many details, too many experiences. The circumstances of the death can make a great difference in the grief period, as can the support systems the grieving person has available.

The loss of one's baby is completely different from the loss of one's parent. The loss of a teenaged child differs greatly from that of a spouse. But no matter what the loss has been, it takes time and heart-wrenching work for the wound to heal.

My psychologist friend compares grief to a body wound. He told me to suppose I received a large gash on my arm. At first I would not even want to look at it. It would be too painful. With grief also we will only glance at it briefly in the beginning and then quickly look away. The first week or so we experience shock and numbness, and the actual wound is not examined at all. At this time we are merely existing, marking time.

But then we are tempted to look at the wound more closely. We allow our thoughts to touch on the death just a tiny bit until the pain overwhelms us and we have to look away again. However, each time we are able to look closer and for longer periods of time. After we become accustomed to looking, we will want to touch the wound ever so gently to see how it feels. As the pain diminishes we will touch it more frequently until at last we accept the fact that we have a wound or a loss. This acceptance begins the recovery period.

At this time it becomes possible to sometimes mention the lost loved one without even crying. We may now be able to begin sorting through clothing and personal items. These tasks may cause great pain, but the pain is a part of the healing process. If the grief is treated properly and worked through rather than sublimated, we will be able to touch, talk about, and accept the wound. At last all that will remain is a scar. This process takes time.

If the wound is covered too quickly or bandaged with tranquilizers or frantic activity, normal healing will not take place. The wound can become infected, festered, and cause physical and emotional problems. Nervous breakdowns, attempted suicides, eating disorders, and ulcers are just a few problems that can result from a loss that is treated improperly. Then the wound may have to be reopened in order for healing to take place.

Much has been written claiming that grief takes a year to run its full cycle. This limitation of time can be a very destructive idea. A widow who was beginning to feel better after six months told me she felt guilty that she did not miss her husband more—"Maybe I didn't love him enough," she said.

Likewise, a mother who was still actively grieving three years after the sudden death of her child was concerned that she was losing her mind. We reassured her that grief knows no time limits. These two women had been hearing too much about "it takes a year to get over the death of a loved one." No two wounds are identical, so the healing rates will differ. Each person's emotional bandage is unique.

Dealing with Memories

The theory that it takes one year to grieve the death of a loved one may have derived from the fact that the first year is especially difficult. Each event is dealt with for the first time. Holidays arrive on schedule as if part of the world had not just caved in. A major question may be how to survive until the first anniversary of the death is reached. This date is often one of the most difficult times. Wounds that were beginning to heal are again forced wide open. However, with a little advance preparation these times can be made more bearable.

People have shared with me a wide variety of methods that have worked successfully for them. Several persons said their families gathered on the anniversary of the death and attended a church service. Some preferred to be alone to walk along the beach or drive through the mountains for quiet reflection and meditation.

For other people projects performed in honor of the loved one and presented on the difficult days brought great comfort. One family grieving the death of a young child embroidered a picture of Jesus with the inscription "Suffer the Little Children to Come unto Me." The picture was presented to their church on the child's birthday and will hang in the nursery in loving memory. They told me that with each stitch they released little David a bit more until the picture was completed and they were ready to remember him with happiness instead of only heartbreaking grief.

The mother of a teenaged girl who was killed in a car accident sorted through her fabric remnants, took swatches of fabric from all the garments she had sewn for her daughter over the years, and made a quilt from them. She called it her "loving memories" quilt. As she assembled it she remembered each article of clothing she had made and the happy occasions when her daughter had worn it. The mother would handle the quilt in times of sorrow and feel her spirits lift.

When we no longer have our loved one to touch, the tactile sense sometimes needs a replacement. My need to touch is so great that I sometimes find myself on my hands and knees at the cemetery, rubbing my dear friend's grave marker. It is the only thing I have left of her to touch. I do not try to control this urge because it puts me in the perfect position to pray.

Making a picture collage is one way of remembering and expressing feelings as snapshots are collected and arranged. Filling a memorabilia box with favorite items that belonged to the loved one is another. Giving a memorial donation and buying flowers for the altar are additional ways in which people express feelings of love and remembrance on special days.

Planting a memorial garden with favorite flowers of the deceased is another therapeutic activity. Working in the garden seems to give great solace to many of us. Something about feeling the raw earth in our bare hands is comforting, and the planting of seeds or flowers has a way of renewing our closeness with nature. It reassures us that life does go on. No matter how barren the soil or how barren our souls, blossoms can be brought forth.

One September I held a daffodil bulb in my hand and thought it looked as dried up, ugly, and dead as I felt. However, I forced myself to sink it into the ground as I brooded over the news of my dad's terminal cancer. The following spring I looked out my kitchen window at that perky yellow flower and remembered the lifeless bulb. *If a lovely flower can appear from such an origin,* I thought, *I can try to produce something beautiful from my father's awful illness.*

Pets are another source of great comfort. They will usually give love unconditionally and rarely mind when their owners are depressed or cranky. Dogs are eager to go for a walk even at midnight. They will curl up in front of the television set for hours on end, no matter how boring the shows. The warmth and love of something living means much to people who are feeling barely alive.

I find that pet owners seem to begin their recovery sooner than other people, if for no other reason than that they feel needed. No matter how listless they are feeling, they are forced out of bed to feed the pets and let them outside. It causes a structuring of each and every day with some semblance of continuity. Getting a rambunctious puppy may be too energetic a project at this time, but animal shelters are filled with plenty of older, calmer pets that also need homes.

Holidays

In addition to our own personal holidays, we must contend with other holidays as well. Thanksgiving Day arrives every single year in November whether we feel we have anything to be thankful for or not.

Immediately after Thanksgiving Day we are confronted full force with the Christmas season. It arrives with the traditional music, fragrances, and decorations. We cannot go anywhere without being made aware that the holiday season is here. Regardless of the way we are feeling, Bing Crosby sings "White Christmas," and the stockings are hung by the chimney with care. All around us the world is in a frenzy of shopping, baking, and activity. We feel as if we are the only ones at a complete standstill in the middle of an alien land. The holiday season accentuates the fact that our loved ones are no longer with us.

To make matters worse, decisions are hurled at us daily. Do we send Christmas cards, put up a Christmas tree, accept dinner invitations? Do we go out of town or stay home? Do we ignore long-standing traditions, begin new ones, or bury our heads under the bedcovers as we want to do? Friends and relatives all have advice and expectations, only adding to the guilt and depression.

Advice, especially, is usually meaningless and empty at this time. Each griever has to work out the best solution for his or her needs. Possible solutions should be weighed carefully to see what fits most comfortably.

An awareness that we are not suffering alone may help somewhat. Many other people also feel isolated from the festivities and alone in a variety of ways. Families split by divorce and families separated by distance have a difficult time handling the holiday season. People with meager financial means who cannot afford to keep up with the demands of the season also struggle to survive. In many households there is sadness, often hidden behind a happy facade.

A season that began as the remembrance of the blessed birth has unfortunately evolved into a season of a high rate of suicides and heavy burdens.

Being aware of this fact and reaching out to help others during this season can often ease our own pain. Serving a holiday dinner at the local mission can help some of us look away from ourselves. Offering to fill in for coworkers on the holiday so they can be at home with their families is another way of reaching out.

Our best insurance is planning ahead instead of letting the holidays catch us unaware. We must think everything through very carefully, weighing all our options so that as we go into battle we have a full armor of protection, an armor of faith, inner strength, happy memories from the past, and hope for the future.

It does not seem to matter so much what is actually done during the difficult days but rather that a plan is devised and carried out. The important part is the advance preparation and being physically rested. Fatigue leaves the emotions raw and makes us more vulnerable.

My gift for the holiday season is three little words: *Don't give up.* As bleak as the winter season of the soul may seem, never has a winter failed to be followed by springtime. Spring may begin with a few false starts or take a long time arriving, but each year, without fail, it does in fact appear. Our souls also experience cold, barren, desolate seasons, but spring will eventually arrive, and daffodils will emerge from dormant bulbs.

Along with the trying days that we can prepare for come some unexpected little events; these seem to be the most difficult. They creep up and take us by surprise because we cannot prepare for them in advance.

One widow told me she felt as if a bayonet had been thrust into her gut and that it was constantly being twisted and turned at strange times. I would describe my own feelings at these moments as similar to being hit in the stomach with a baseball. It knocked the wind out of me and made me gasp aloud.

A mother whose son had been very patriotic felt devastated after seeing the flags lined up on Main Street on Flag Day. Another woman said she cried every Sunday. When questioned about it she flatly stated, "I guess I cry because Sunday is as good a day for crying as any." Grief does not know about rhyme or reason; it simply happens.

The Sense of Loss

C. S. Lewis states in *A Grief Observed* that one will get over grief but will never be the same. "To say the patient is getting over it after an operation for appendicitis is one thing; after he's had his leg [cut] off is quite another."[3] In the beginning, the gaping wound or the stump will be tremendously painful. Stitches of love, support, happy memories, and faith in God will pull the wound together to make it hurt less.

As the pain subsides, the patient may be given a prosthesis and learn to walk quite efficiently with it. He may even compensate for his loss by going on to experience greater feats than he would have before the amputation. However, he will never forget that he once had two legs. One man told me he would rather have had his right arm amputated than have lost his wife.

With enough time only the scar will remain. The scar can serve as a reminder of the intense healing that once occurred. Eventually, looking at the scar will bring about a slight feeling of satisfaction, and we may be able to say, *Yes, I did survive this horrendous wound, and I am still intact.*

TWO

The Flood

At first being intact is all that matters. We can wrap grief around us like a cocoon. The numbness helps until eventually it is tempting to peek out of the cocoon and lightly touch the hurt. When we do, we are shocked by the intensity of the pain and the acute aloneness. By this time the support of family and friends is probably beginning to wear thin.

We can sense that we are expected to get on with life. But what life? What is there to be "gotten on with"? Nothing is the same anymore, and we are unable to pick up the pieces after we have been shattered into tiny fragments. Often we are not only missing our loved ones, we are also missing other support systems that seem to have vanished. In our despair we feel no one understands.

The truth is, no one does. Death makes most people terribly uncomfortable. Friends do not know what to do or what to say. Some people speak to us in clichés at this time, our least favorite words to hear. Eventually they may find it easier to stay away, using the excuse that they do not want to cause any additional anguish.

Often when we are visiting with friends or relatives and no one mentions the deceased person, we may wonder if the person did in fact exist. When we do mention the missing loved one we notice a hush spreading over the room. All conversation stops. Now is when anger and depression can enter the scene. *Maybe the numbness was better after all,* we may think.

A remedy that members of our bereavement group found successful in this social situation was gently telling friends or family how they felt. Honesty seemed to work best.

One member used this example: "It makes me feel so much better when I talk about _____. I know I get teary when we do this, but it is still better than not talking about her at all. I hope it doesn't make you feel too awkward."

It seems unfair that in addition to the suffering we have to be the ones to educate others, but such openness can save valuable relationships. People do not act inconsiderately on purpose. What appears as thoughtlessness and cruelty to us is actually the discomfort and misinformation of others.

The Stages of Grief

Grief work can be divided into five basic stages that most grieving people experience. These stages do not have to be in any particular order, and they can be repeated. Merely knowing that there are defined stages and recognizing them can bring comfort. It is reassuring to know that these stages are normal occurrences in a world where nothing seems normal any longer.

Grief is the process of coming to terms with the changes that take place when a loved one is removed from our lives. Each of the stages is a step along the path to recovery.

The first stage commonly experienced is shock. As the numbness from the shock wears off, sighing replaces the stabs of pain. Along with the shock and sighing is the most necessary of the stages, crying. It would be a mistake to try to hold back tears. They are a language that expresses anguish in a way words cannot.

The most confusing of the stages is anger. It is often experienced with a frightening, new intensity, causing guilt to hide around every corner, creeping up frequently. In addition to these stages, the feeling of depression hovers in between, stands beside, and moves around constantly.

1. Shock

In the beginning, shock and numbness are necessary and welcome. The mind will accept only what it is capable of handling. Shock allows us to calmly hear devastating news and still function. It carries us through the first agonizing minutes until we can begin to absorb the horrendous news.

One afternoon I received a phone call notifying me that my uncle had just suffered a fatal coronary. I calmly asked for all the details, wrote down the information, and thanked the caller before hanging up the phone. No other relatives lived within hundreds of miles so I was responsible for all the initial arrangements. Shock had allowed me to accept the original phone call.

I took a few deep breaths before calling my daughter to tell her the bad news. As I began to talk to her the reality of the words I was about to say hit me so violently that I could no longer speak.

Numbness helped me carry on during the following week. It allowed me to participate in the wake, the funeral Mass, and the proper military burial complete with a bugler off in the distance playing taps.

A few weeks later, after the tasks were completed, the numbness wore off, and I realized I could no longer pick up the phone and talk to a very special person who had been there for me my entire life. I began to grieve.

The passage of time allowed the wound to heal a bit before I touched it. I grasped as much pain as I could and then turned it off. At first it would have been unwise to force the wound open any wider and intensify the agony. With time it was possible to gradually accept the loss.

2. Sighing

The sighing stage that Joyce Huggett mentions in *Growing into Love* (InterVarsity Press, 1984) is similar to the deep breathing techniques that are taught in stress management classes. Sighing is a natural way to relax the body and release stress.

Grieving people are in a high-tension, high-stress state. Their breathing is often fast and shallow, thus not getting enough oxygen to their blood. Poorly oxygenated blood contributes to anxiety, stress, depression, and fatigue. Digestion is hampered. Good, healthy sighs can help to relieve this condition and in fact make a person feel more relaxed physically and mentally.

3. Crying

Crying is essential. The deep sobbing previously mentioned is usually followed by months of crying floods of tears. It would be close to impossible and unnatural to not release tears after experiencing the loss of a loved one.

The Bible describes tears often. We are told that God collects our tears in a bottle and keeps track of every one of them (Ps. 56:8). And in Psalm 84:6 we read: "When they walk through the Valley of Weeping it will become a place of springs where pools of blessing and refreshment collect after rains!" If all the tears a grieving person shed could be saved, they would indeed make pools—pools that would quite likely bring about blessings someday. These tears are cleansing a deep wound.

Studies are being done on the tears of the grieving because some scientists believe that tears may contain chemicals that actually relieve stress in the body. If this possibility is proven true, we can claim that tears not only feel soothing but are actually changing the body chemistry to a more comfortable state.

When one of my favorite aunts was dying, I sat holding her hand and praying for her. My tears fell onto her limp hand. Moments later she took her last breath, while my tears were still wet on her hand. I felt as if a baptism had taken place, a cleansing of sorts, of the love she would take from this world to her new home. I have received great comfort from the picture of her hand at that moment.

Tears come to my eyes and a lump to my throat as I recall this memory. Sometimes my tears embarrass me, and I need to remind myself that they are natural, normal, and healing. They calm me and remind me of the good times we shared before that last memory.

4. Anger

Angry feelings arrive with a shocking force following the death of a loved one. We may ask ourselves questions such as these: *How can I be so angry when I hurt so much? How can I be angry at the loved one who has died?* or *How can I be angry with God?*

No one is alone in this anger. A widow in our bereavement group, whose husband had been killed when his snowmobile rolled over on top of him, told us that six months later she still stood at the window, where she had watched the accident, and shook her fist at her husband. *I told you that vehicle was dangerous and you shouldn't drive it so fast! Now look what you've gone and done!* she said under her breath.

Her anger was justified. She did not want to spend her retirement years alone. She and her husband had planned to travel. He was sixty years old and in excellent health when he died. He had been driving the snowmobile recklessly when he went into a skid and lost control. To not be angry would be unrealistic.

The mother of a teenaged boy who was killed in a motorcycle accident said, "I'm so angry, but I have no one to take it out on. I'm furious with God, and that is sacrilegious. I'm angry at Billy, and he isn't here anymore. Where can my anger go?"

Anger this intense has to go somewhere. However, it must not be directed at a remaining spouse or children. Nor should it be directed at clerks, service workers, or neighbors.

Often our anger is directed at God. This realization can be very frightening. We are ashamed to admit that we are angry at God, yet when we do, we find that others feel the same way. If we have served God faithfully we feel we have been rejected and abused. *Why me, Lord?* becomes a recurrent theme.

We wonder if we are being punished for the sins of our parents or for our own wrongdoing. I believe that heartaches result from living in this imperfect world where we have been given free will from God. God, as our father, wants only what is best for us.

So where can we channel this anger? At our bereavement group we suggested that the angry mother take an old pillow and a tennis racket to a deserted place. There she could shout, cry, and beat the pillow to pieces. She took our advice, returning the next week to report that she not only burst the pillow and scattered feathers all over but also broke the tennis racket in three places. When she finished, she threw down the last piece of the racket, brushed her hands together in an "all finished" gesture, and strode home with her head held high.

She may have to repeat this exercise from time to time as the anger resurfaces. Anger that is bottled up will explode at inappropriate times or will be turned inward and become depression. Releasing it at scheduled times will prevent uncontrolled eruptions. After anger, guilt arrives, followed by depression, the worst symptom of all to eliminate.

5. Depression

We recognize depression in those who feel that no joy is left in life, that there is little hope circumstances will improve, and that getting through each moment requires effort. Depression is certainly normal for anyone who is grieving, but if it seems to go on endlessly it can be an indication of a more serious condition. If thoughts of suicide keep creeping in or if there is no desire to live week after endless week, then the depression will need to be confronted.

Depression can be the result of grief that is held inside, tears that go unshed, or feelings that are not expressed. Psychologists claim that we are the best judge of our own depression. If the reply to the question *How depressed am I?* is *It seems like a normal amount that can be expected under the circumstances,* the situation is all right. If the answer is, *I'm depressed beyond belief and it never lets up,* it might be time to join a support group or talk to a professional counselor.

A great amount of depression is the result of negative internal dialogue or the tapes we play in our heads. When I first heard this statement from an instructor I was quite skeptical. Surely I didn't talk to myself or "hear tapes"! When I began to listen to myself I was appalled at what I heard. Alcoholics Anonymous calls it "stinkin' thinkin'" and I could readily identify with it. I found I was thinking negative, depressing thoughts continually.

I would get up in the morning and say "I feel awful," or "I can tell it's going to be one of those days." I was constantly thinking, *I can't do this, I'll never finish, I can't handle this,* and *I'm so depressed.*

My most destructive thought was, *Why me?* My very soul was plagued with those two little words. With my thoughts centered inward, I could do nothing but feel sorry for myself. I could make no positive moves. In order to feel better I had to change my thinking from *Why me?* to *What can I do with this?* I needed to look outside my wretched self. At that point the dark curtains of depression parted a bit and allowed the light to trickle in.

What can we do about depression? First we must recognize it. Depression can wear many different masks. It can come disguised in bouts of insomnia, extreme fatigue, withdrawal from other people, loss of appetite, or a complete lack of interest in life.

Insomnia

When we are grieving, nights seem long, dark, and desolate. Even after we get to the point where we can cope with the days, the nights still hover bleakly above us. Because it is essential to be well rested, sleep problems should be dealt with as soon as possible. Sleeping pills and alcohol are not a good solution and can become more of a problem than the original insomnia.

The best way to deal with insomnia is to experiment. For some people, drinking a cup of hot chocolate at bedtime, reading until tired, taking a relaxing bath in the evening, or listening to soothing music may be helpful. Other people may find health products beneficial. Health food stores carry a wide variety of herbal teas blended specifically to calm and soothe. Calcium supplements taken at bedtime have been found to aid in relaxation.

I choose to read my Bible and spend some quiet time in prayer prior to turning out the lights. I usually fall asleep immediately but awaken three or four hours later and feel wide awake. At that time I will get up, have a glass of milk and a couple of crackers, and then settle down again in the dark to resume my prayer time. I usually fall asleep before I get to the end of my prayer requests.

It is best to stay away from stimulating activities before bedtime such as exercising, talking on the phone, or watching high-key shows on television.

As with many other aspects of grief, there is no easy solution to the sleeping problems. With time and experimentation, each person will probably find a successful means of coping. What works for one person may not necessarily work for another. What works this week may not work next week. Some people find it helpful to take short naps during the day in order to obtain enough rest.

Problems with Appetite

Another disturbing part of grief is that overweight people tend to overeat and underweight people lose their appetites. It is unfortunate that it does not work in the reverse.

Good nutrition is important at all times. Now is no time to begin a rigorous diet to lose weight. It is also not the time to overeat chocolate or donuts.

Just like proper sleep, proper nutrition can contribute to a feeling of well-being. When one already feels awful it is especially important not to form any additional negative habits.

Taking Care of Yourself

The best antidepressants do not come in a bottle; they come in a lifestyle of practicing good eating habits, getting adequate sleep, and taking proper care of ourselves. The grief period is a time when pampering ourselves is not a luxury but an absolute necessity. For some strange reason we Americans have developed a way of life that frowns on spoiling ourselves. We think we must be at peak performance or we feel guilty. To turn off the phone in the afternoon and take a nap is considered disgraceful, and to soak in a luxurious bath filled with bubbles is thought to be overindulgent.

Doing the things we enjoy can be very beneficial. We will have no desire to exert the energy to do these things, so we will have to force ourselves.

Talking about our problems is an excellent release for depression. Trying to put a blanket over our feelings does not smother the fire within. It merely covers it, allowing it to smolder inside until the embers are fanned into full force again.

Facing the Pain

Grief will hurt whether or not we face it. We might manage to delay or repress it until it appears in severe physical ailments or some other form, but it will not disappear. Either way grief is painful. By facing it, we are eventually able to feel better.

Harold S. Kushner, in *When Bad Things Happen to Good People,* tells us that scientists have determined ways for measuring pain. They claim that two of the most painful human experiences are the passing of a kidney stone and giving birth.

However, the difference is in the type of pain. Passing a kidney stone is a horrendous experience while giving birth is an act of love and a creative experience. Those who have passed kidney stones say they never want to go through the experience again; but most women who have endured the pain of childbirth will gladly have more than one child.

Pain is the price we pay for being alive. Dead cells—our hair, our fingernails—can't feel pain: they cannot feel anything. When we understand that, our question will change from, "Why do we have to feel pain?" to "What do we do with our pain so that it becomes meaningful and not just pointless empty suffering? How can we turn all the painful experiences of our lives into birth pangs or into growing pains?" We may not ever understand why we suffer or be able to control the forces that cause our suffering but we can have a lot to say about what the suffering does to us, and what sort of people we become because of it. Pain makes some people bitter and envious. It makes others sensitive and compassionate. It is the result, not the cause of the pain that makes some experiences of pain meaningful and others empty and destructive.[1]

Will the pain we suffer from our loss be productive or will it destroy the rest of our lives?

Making Decisions

In the early stages of grief it is unwise to make any major decisions or changes in lifestyle. During this time a person is often incapable of thinking clearly, and extra disorientation adds unnecessary stress.

Selling a house or moving in with relatives should be postponed for at least a year. Changing jobs, marrying, getting a divorce, having a baby, and moving are usually all too vital to tackle competently. If at all possible, these decisions and any other major ones should be postponed until grief is fully recognized and accepted.

An exception to this rule is in regard to the base of support. For example, if a couple has retired to Phoenix from Los Angeles just before the wife dies, the base of support for the husband might still be in Los Angeles. In that case a move to return to the place where friends and family can offer the most support might be wise.

Laughter

Some people may think laughter has no place in grieving. Indeed it does! Society makes us feel guilty if we are acting frivolous following a funeral, but human beings can use laughter as a release from stress. The mind and body have limits to the anguish they can withstand. When facing the loss of a loved one, laughter can remove the cork from the bottle and allow some of the pain to bubble out.

Several years ago, when my husband and I were standing alone in front of his mother's casket, we shared a few loving memories. One of the memories brought laughter to our hearts, and as we stood with hands clutched together for comfort, we began to laugh. Anyone looking on this scene from a distance must have been horrified at our laughter, but to us it made the trip to the cemetery a bit more bearable.

Our bereavement group laughs often. Our grieving experiences are too intense to be endured twenty-four hours a day. Ann laughed when she told us that her dog ate the only copy of her income tax return on April 12. She admitted that she had not laughed when it actually happened, but a few days later she was able to see some humor in it.

Diane told us she could not find her favorite tennis shoes after her husband's funeral. We all had a good laugh when she reported back that they had turned up in her freezer! We told her rumor had it she was getting cold feet.

A humorous book in small doses or a comical show or movie at the right time can do wonders for lifting moods. Scientific studies have been made between groups in hospitals who had similar illnesses. One group was subjected to laughter on a regular basis, and the other group was not. The group that laughed recovered at a much speedier rate.

With laughter, endorphins are released within the body and act as a healing agent, making the body feel physically and emotionally better.

Support

When we are grieving we will need crutches. Crutches have a bad reputation, often bearing a negative connotation. I would like to dispute this assumption. A person with a broken leg would be very foolish to try to walk without the help of a crutch.

Not all crutches are made of wood or metal. A person with a broken spirit would also be foolish to try to function without a crutch. I have heard that religion is merely a crutch and so are support groups. If they are crutches, then I am grateful that they are available to lean on while we mend.

I have a divine best friend who loves me no matter what, who understands my every need, who is with me every single moment, and who wants to share my heavy load. This friend, Jesus, is available to everyone through prayer.

Churches are usually the most supportive places to turn when we are grieving. They offer Bible study groups and worship services and minister to people in a variety of other ways.

Bereavement groups are another means of support. If none exists in a given community, a few phone calls might help start one. Possibly the Chamber of Commerce, Visiting Nurses, or another community group would take on the project. I am not suggesting that a grieving person try to start one; it would be too difficult to do so with eyes still blurred with tears.

At bereavement support group meetings grieving persons meet with others who understand what they are experiencing. When regular attendees at these meetings say "I know just how you feel," newcomers know they truly do. Because they have the same hurts and feel the same fears, their tears mingle together to provide a soothing balm for the spirit. They also share solutions. I have seen grieving hearts stretch and stretch to embrace the pain of others and in doing so release a bit of their own agony.

As time passes, the search for hope continues unnoticed until one day for a brief time the bereaved person may see a glimpse of sunlight piercing a rain cloud. Hope will become a reality during this fleeting moment as a rainbow appears on the horizon.

THREE

The Rainbow

Having lived in a desert climate for over twenty years, I consider a rainbow a rare and wonderful sight. It is not only a colorful arc in the sky caused by the refraction and reflection of sun rays in droplets of water but also a promise from God that he will never again destroy all humanity. With that promise comes the message of approval to begin life anew.

The Healing Process

Four tasks aid in the grief process:

1. Facing the reality of the loss (Letting go)
2. Experiencing the pain of grief (Crying and talking about it)
3. Adjusting to the altered environment (Acceptance)
4. Reinvesting emotional energy elsewhere (Reaching out)

On November 28, 1942, a fire broke out in Boston's famous nightclub, the Coconut Grove, causing 493 deaths. Many of the six hundred survivors were severely burned. In the hospital identical methods of treatment were used, yet some patients' burns healed and others did not.

Because many of the patients were also grieving the loss of loved ones who had been at the nightclub with them during the tragedy, physicians began to suspect that emotional and mental attitudes might be making the difference in the healing process.

Psychiatrists were called in to assist, and some of the first research and studies on grief were begun at that time. Among the psychiatrists was Dr. Erich Lindemann, who went on to make great strides in helping the bereaved. His research showed that there was a definite correlation between the expression of grief and the successful healing of physical wounds. He also discovered that the healing of outside wounds corresponded with the healing of the entire person.

The patients who were healing successfully were the ones who were facing their grief openly. They shed abundant tears, talked about their loss and hurt, and expressed guilt over surviving when their loved ones had not. They recalled the terror of the incident and their fright at the time. When the thoughts became too painful they turned away from them for a while but then returned to gradually work through them. They allowed themselves to think and talk about their lost loved ones, recalling happy memories of the love and happiness they had shared together.

The patients whose burns were not healing were the ones who refused to talk about the tragedy. They pretended it had never happened or said it was too painful for them to think or talk about. They rarely shed any tears. They put up a brave front, keeping their emotions locked inside. They had no hope that they would ever recover or feel better.

Lindemann found the people who were not facing grief openly showed all the signs of depression and often ex–

pressed displaced anger, bitterness, and resentment toward doctors, city officials, firefighters, or the nightclub owners.

Other ways of avoiding grief are extensive traveling, staying tremendously busy, or taking drugs or alcohol to produce a false sense of calm. Escape methods of this sort soon backfire. Physical symptoms appear, depression persists, or the grief is greatly intensified.

Lindemann's final conclusions were that grief must be faced relentlessly, no matter how painful, to enable emotional wounds to heal. His research showed the necessity of feeling the hurt, the loneliness, and the anguish until it becomes thoroughly familiar. Then, and only then, can it be accepted as a part of life.[1]

At that time it can be used as a starting point to reorganize a new life. This process is considered successful grief work, approaching the point where life can be started anew.

Letting Go of Grief

Often letting go of our grief becomes confused with letting go of our loved one. While our grief is fresh we feel as if we have something to hold close to us. We fear letting go of the grief, subconsciously thinking then we will have nothing. At first even the grief is better than nothing.

I have seen homes where parents kept their child's bedroom as a shrine for years after the child has died. I have seen a widow's home where the slippers belonging to her deceased husband were still under the bed five years after his death. These examples are extreme cases of not letting go. As long as the changes have not been made and the grief is kept alive, the survivors can pretend the person will be returning.

Often in these cases the deceased is placed on a pedestal, made into a saint. Reality is completely distorted. The first step in working through grief is to let go. That does not mean to let go of the happy memories or to dispose of every single item the person ever owned.

It means to be reasonable. It is certainly reasonable to display favorite photos and to keep special belongings. It is even reasonable to wear clothing that belonged to the deceased, but not every minute of every single day.

Healing can begin as the survivor takes care of legalities such as changing names on deeds or bank accounts, bringing insurance policies up to date, and filing a death certificate.

In cleaning closets and sorting personal items to save or give away, the survivor moves along in the grief process. If absolutely nothing has been touched by the six-month anniversary, it might be a good idea for the person to seek professional help or have a close friend or relative help begin these tasks. By this time most surviving persons have begun the sorting and giving away. Many things cannot be parted with yet but at least the task has been started.

At this time memories can be helpful or harmful. If we allow ourselves to be saddened by every picture or memory, we will become more bogged down with depression. If, instead, we allow the memories to fill us with happiness over the times we shared, then we can carry this gift always.

My friend Lynn's father died suddenly while all their belongings were in storage awaiting the completion of a new home. Several months later when the house was finished, Lynn helped her mother move. Unpacking was a time of great sadness, moving without the mate who had so carefully planned the special house.

As they opened box after box of items packed lovingly by her dad, Lynn began to wonder how they would ever complete the heartbreaking task. Lynn decided she would have to turn her thoughts into something positive. As she and her mom handled each item Lynn attached a happy memory to it.

"Mom, remember when Dad and I used to bring you breakfast in bed and we used this coffee server? We would giggle as we tried to work quietly in the kitchen so you would be surprised. And this baseball—how Daddy liked to toss it to our puppy!"

As they continued to handle the items the former tears were replaced with laughter. Lynn told me she discovered the choice was hers when it came to memories. "The memories can bring me sadness over my loss or they can bring me the joy of remembering. Daddy would want me to choose laughter over tears, and so I try to do that," she said. It seemed a good choice to me too!

Dealing with Paperwork

Even as the first signs of hope appear, the new way of life will be accompanied by many frustrations. Events that were a mere inconvenience before the death will now seem like gigantic immovable objects because dealing with the loss of a loved one takes every ounce of strength and energy. Dealing with grief pushes us to maximum capacity, and anything extra puts us into overload. The little daily problems will seem enormous and throw us into a tailspin. When this happens we may need to stop, reassess, and use some of the techniques discussed earlier.

As we venture back into the world we will be faced with the reality of paperwork. There will be mountains of unpaid bills, insurance forms, thank-you notes to write, and letters to answer. Every day the mail will bring more stacks until we feel as if we will never get caught up. As the piles grow higher, we become so discouraged we scarcely know where to begin.

The best way to deal with all this paperwork is dividing the correspondence into categories according to importance. By setting reasonable goals, we are not as likely to get frustrated or discouraged. Giving ourselves a reward each day after we have met a goal can help. Eventually the pile will diminish and not seem overwhelming.

Asking for Help

Murphy's Law applies especially to the grieving because anything that can go wrong at this time will. The water pipes will freeze, the dog will eat the income tax form, a bird will get stuck in the chimney, and the car will, without a doubt, break down.

Our bereavement group has a "share-a-disaster" night from time to time, and every person has at least one story to tell. The stories often become humorous as people share them, and this relieves some of the distress.

When disasters hit, we are better off sharing them with a friend or relative before they have a chance to destroy any progress we may have been making. We shouldn't be afraid to ask for help.

Most people do not know what to say or do for the grieving. Therefore, these occasions are opportunities to educate them. We can let them know that we would appreciate help in practical matters.

Another request we need to make is for hugs. In her delightful book *Hug Therapy*, Kathleen Keating states, "Touch is not only nice. It's needed. Scientific research supports the theory that stimulation by touch is absolutely necessary for our physical as well as our emotional well being."[2]

While there are many ways of touching, hugging is one of the best. We should not hesitate to tell a friend, "I need a hug!" Strangers would probably be happy to accommodate us too, but it is more advisable to take this liberty only with friends and relatives. I ask for hugs often and have never yet been turned down.

A personal friend who is a psychologist claims that people need four hugs a day just as preventative maintenance. He says seven hugs are absolutely required for good mental health. So rather than take the chance of running a deficit, I keep close count and try never to go below my daily quota. Carrying over from day to day is frowned on.

Hug Therapy is worthwhile reading that will cause a smile, and smiles are good too.

The Final Stage of Grief—Acceptance

The final stage of grief is reorganization or acceptance. To begin to form new traditions, change our goals, and look ahead aids recovery. Deceased loved ones will always leave voids in our lives and will continue to be missed; nevertheless, it is possible for life to be good again. Moments of sadness will wash over us forever, but between those moments can be daily successes. We need to begin to set new goals. These goals need not be enormous challenges. They can be small practical things such as learning to operate the lawn mower or balance the checkbook, rewarded with a pat on the back for reorganizing and accomplishing a new goal.

A friend told me the phrase "life after death" has taken on a new meaning since the death of her husband. She asks, "Is there a life for me after his death?"

At first it seemed to her that there was not, and she did not even care. Then, as the numbness and shock wore off, she began to respond again. The first feelings were ones of extreme agony, but with them came a hint that she now cared about the quality of her life.

She remembered how it felt to be happy, and she wanted to feel like that again. However, trying to figure out the way to feel better took too much effort in the beginning. She discovered that talking about her distress helped ease it a tiny bit. A single ray of sunshine flashing through her life would give her hope.

Unlike the bumper sticker that states "Once I gave up hope things got better," feeling hopeless was definitely not better for my friend. It was the very lowest of valleys. She desired to leave the Valley of Weeping and move toward the light at the top of the mountain. She wanted a life after death here on earth.

1. Growing

When I visited Pikes Peak I looked at valleys with new insight. The valley at the bottom of the mountain was lush and green with dense foliage. We boarded a cable car for the trip to the top of the mountain, passing mountain streams, waterfalls, and spectacular views of the valley.

Then all of a sudden I looked out the window and saw nothing but rocks of various shapes, colors, and sizes. We were above the timberline near the top of Pikes Peak, which is 14,110 feet high. The air is clear, and the view is indescribably beautiful. However, nothing grows up there. For all its peace and beauty, it is barren and fruitless.

Fay Angus wisely says:

If we lived only on the mountaintops of life, our souls would be barren. It is in the deep and low places, often the places hidden from everyone but God; it is in the valleys of our sorrows and our griefs that we cultivate . . . understanding, compassion, courage, sensitivity, sympathy, kindness and all those tender mercies.[3]

The mountaintop may be quiet and peaceful, a restful place to be, but growth takes place only in the valleys. As we face our grief and acknowledge it, we are growing. The ache of our loss and our loneliness will act as fertilizer for our souls. But in order to reap any kind of harvest we have to

reach out and begin life anew with the crop we have culti-
vated. Angus further observes, "Successful grief plants jon-
quils in the winter season of the heart and waits to see them
burst to life with reassurance of the spring."[4]

2. Reaping

What we plant is exactly what we will reap. This principle
is illustrated in a story of a little girl with a nasty older sister
who teased and tormented her relentlessly. One day after
such an episode the little sister ran away crying. She ran
through the woods to a hill behind her house and stood sobbing on the hilltop, filled with anger at her older sister.

"I hate you!" she shouted and heard a voice holler back at
her, "I hate you!"

She ran, very frightened, back home where she found her
mother.

"Mommy, a terrible monster is out past the woods, and
he hates me!"

The mother thought for a moment and then smiled. She
took the little girl's hand in hers and said, "Come with me."

They walked through the woods to the hilltop. There the
mother said, "Just tell the terrible monster that you love him."

"I love you," the little girl said softly.

"Shout it out good and loud," the mother told her.

So she did. And the monster answered, "I love you."

Life echoes back whatever we give out. If we show hate-
fulness, that is what we will receive. Conversely, if we dis-
pense comfort, love, tenderness, sympathy, and understanding, that is what we will receive.

3. Reaching Out

Giant redwoods in the Sequoia National Forest reach so
high above my head that I can barely see the tops. The giant

sequoia is one of the oldest and largest living things on earth. The trees grow straight and tall, one next to another, reaching heights of three hundred feet in spite of their shallow roots. Some of these mighty redwoods have stood for three thousand years, withstanding earthquakes, rainstorms, and ferocious winds. The forest rangers claim that the reason the trees are able to survive such stress is that they grow in groves, entwining their shallow roots with each other to make themselves sturdy and strong. One tree alone could never survive; neither can one person.

We ask those members of our bereavement group who are ready to reach out to grasp the hand of a new member and become that person's support system, leading him along the path they have already traveled or helping her to find her way. Rewards are equally shared between the givers and the recipients.

Following the initial period of grief we may see the dim outline of a rainbow reflected through our tears. When we begin shedding those tears for others and not always for ourselves, we know our personal pain will be decreasing. We are then able to look beyond our own loss and become tuned in to others who need us.

At one of our meetings a mother attending for the first time shared the details of her six-year-old son's tragic death. As she completed the heartbreaking story every person in the room was crying. An elderly gentleman took her hand and said between sobs, "Today we weep for you, not ourselves." I knew at that moment our group's healing had begun. It is my prayer that our own hearts never become so tough that we cannot feel the suffering of another and shed tears of sorrow for them.

As we begin to reach out of our own grief we will find that every community needs volunteers. It is a matter of looking for what is most appealing to particular people and situations. Most communities offer classes or have groups that can be joined through churches or other organizations. The important point is to focus on an interest and a goal. By using our grief to help others we will actually be helping ourselves. I was once told, "If you don't like your lot in life, try building a service station."

One woman from our group joined an organization that trains therapy dogs that are taken into convalescent homes and classrooms for mentally and physically handicapped children in the community.

Another woman helps with the Welcome Wagon and meets new residents, helping them adjust to the unfamiliar environment. We have a Girl Scout leader, a budding artist, a karate student, and a poet. Each person is either reaching out to others who are grieving or developing a new interest.

In the reorganizing of life we will clearly see a rainbow in the distance. Rainbows are fleeting; they are faint and fragile, just as the first glimpse of hope will be. But then the sun will burst from behind the clouds to shine brightly down on us.

The sun will warm not only our bodies but also our hearts, until the day when joy begins to grow again. Our lives may never be the same but they need not be without love, peace, or happiness.

Grief Exercises

Research has shown that the most effective way for grievers to ease their pain is through talking about their situation. However, many grievers claim that a few weeks after the funeral people no longer seem to want to listen to them. That leaves them with intense emotions bottled up inside.

Support groups can help fill the need to share, as can keeping a journal on your thoughts and feelings. The following practical exercises may guide the direction of your thoughts and assist you along the path toward complete healing.

Let the questions guide you as you walk down the unfamiliar road of grief. Use a notebook to fill in your answers and date your entries so you can check back periodically to review your progress. Do not rush your journey; plan to do each step slowly, giving yourself time to absorb it. It is important to do some deep thinking about your situation and to move forward only when you feel ready.

Grief is not just a process, it is work—extremely hard work. The mere passage of time without hard work will not complete the process; it will only delay it. Grievers may find themselves still at square one if they have not allowed themselves time to work through their grief.

Nevertheless, I am aware that people cannot heal their own wounds. Only with God's guidance is it possible to recover from grief. Begin your writing exercises with prayer and let the Lord be your guide.

Beginning the Journey of Grief

1. Compare your grief to a wound. How are the two similar? Where are you in the healing process right now?
2. List some of the clichés people have said to you regarding your grief. (Example: "Time heals all wounds.")
3. Write down how these comments made you feel.

Feelings

It is important to be aware of your feelings so you can concentrate on dealing with them. To help identify your feelings, answer the following questions.

Are you feeling fearful?

Are you in shock?

Do you feel guilty?

Do you cry frequently?

Are you angry?

Are you depressed?

Are you lonely?

Do you feel confused?

Are you out of control?

Do you have any physical ailments?

Are you suffering from anxiety?

1. Ask yourself, "How am I feeling right now?" and list your feelings.
2. What bandages, if any, have you placed on your wound?
3. What can you do in the next few days to better treat your wound and allow healing?
4. What about in the next few weeks?

Take a look at your list and use it as a reference for identifying feelings. Even though your feelings may change rapidly, the list can serve as a guideline. In addition to the following information, reread the sections in the book on the specific feelings you are experiencing.

Guilt and unforgiveness are two areas that can cause severe suffering. Use the following exercises to address them.

Guilt

Guilt will stand in the way of complete healing. When feelings of guilt are eating away at you, you cannot move forward.

1. Make a list of any guilty feelings you may be harboring (usually indicated by statements that begin with *If only, What if, I should have,* or *Why didn't I*).
2. Start with the first item on your list and ask yourself these three questions:

   • Is my guilt realistic?
   • Can I change it?
   • Do I need to make amends with someone in order to remove the guilt?

Continue to ask the same three questions for each item on your list.

Sometimes, guilt is legitimate. If you discover this to be true after answering the previously mentioned questions, you may have to do some soul-searching to try to find positive ways to balance the scales. One way to approach this might be to do the following.

1. Picture a seesaw. One side is guilt; one side is a good deed. Have the guilty side touching the ground.
2. Place good deeds and happy memories on the other side. Keep adding to these until that side touches the ground, leaving the guilty side up in the air.
3. Forgive yourself for your mistakes and use them as a point of growth.

Forgiveness

1. Think about any areas in your life where forgiveness is necessary. Write a brief summary of each situation—include who, what, and why.
2. Write a plan for the way you will begin to weed out any unforgiveness in your life.
3. Are you holding onto unforgiveness toward yourself? How can you resolve it?
4. Are you blaming someone else for your loss? If so, write a letter explaining your thoughts and feelings. The letter does not have to be mailed, simply written.

Holidays and Special Days

Along with all the other symptoms and feelings of grief there is the added burden of holidays or special dates. The most important thing you can do prior to such occasions is to come up with a plan.

1. Are any particular dates more difficult than others? Write down these dates so you can have them in front of you and not be caught unprepared when they arrive.
2. Write down a tentative plan for the next special date that is coming up.
3. Sketch out as many of the details as you can before that day arrives.
4. Ask yourself these questions in regard to your plan:

   • Do I feel comfortable with my plan?
   • Do I need to make some changes in it?
   • Do I need to inform anyone else of these plans?
   • Will this new plan be upsetting to others?

5. Once you have worked out a plan, take time to picture the occasion and go over the details in your mind.

Talk to family members about these plans and get their input. Make sure everyone is comfortable with the changes or new traditions, and record their ideas on how the special day should be observed.

Grief is like a roller coaster ride with lots of ups and downs. Realizing this will help you to better handle the various stages in your journey.

Easing the Pain of Grief

1. What was your first reaction to your loss? Think about it before moving on to the next question.
2. Write down any of the details you may remember in regard to the early days of your loss and your feelings of shock.

As you move out of shock, a period of intense pain usually surfaces. The following suggestions may help ease this pain.

Relaxing

In addition to deep sighs, other relaxation measures can also bring about a feeling of peace. Even if you are not conscious of feeling anxious or stressed, chances are you are operating in a high-stress mode.

- Are you more forgetful than usual?
- Do you lose your temper easily?
- Do you have trouble making decisions?
- Do little problems seem to throw you for a loop?

If you answered yes to any of the above questions, you are probably overly stressed, and stress is unhealthy.

1. List some stressful areas in your life. Write down some ways to correct them.
2. Are there any stressors you can remove from your life—even little ones like oiling a squeaky door?

Take time out to relax. Listen to soothing music, learn deep-breathing exercises, soak in a hot tub filled with bubbles, or try other methods that you have found relaxing in the past.

Crying

Tears are a way of expressing ourselves when words are inadequate. They are a stress reliever and a means to recovery. They are not something to cause embarrassment. We should never have to apologize for our tears; they are human, natural, and perfectly normal.

1. If you have not had a deep, cleansing cry since the death of your loved one, allow yourself to do that now. If you have been holding back too long, you might need to trigger your feelings. Look at old photographs or listen to music that will allow you to reflect and feel the many emotions you are experiencing at this time.

2. Write about your feelings toward people who cry. What has been your personal experience with people's reactions when you cry?

Dealing with Anger

Anger is a very real emotion and is frequently connected with grief. Evaluate your personal anger.

1. Are you aware of any angry feelings? Are you angry at God or at your loved one for leaving you? How about the doctors who cared for your loved one? Are you angry at anyone else, including yourself? Has anyone in particular let you down?

2. Write down the name of someone you are feeling angry with right now.

There are three positive ways to deal with feelings of any type: writing, exercising, and talking. Use these tools to relieve anger.

1. Write to release any angry thoughts you might have. Write fast and furiously if necessary. If you are angry with someone who is no longer alive, take the time right now to write a letter that expresses your feelings. It is harmful to keep angry feelings pent up inside.

2. Use some form of physical exercise to release your anger. Choose one that appeals to you. The purpose is to lessen your frustration and begin to feel more relaxed.
3. Talk about your anger. If you are not part of a support group, find someone who is gentle and understanding and who is willing to listen. Tell this person about your anger and that you need to express it to get rid of it. Explain that you aren't looking for answers or solutions, you simply need to expel it.

Defeating Depression

Depression is another stage of grief. Unfortunately, it does not go away by itself; if ignored, it will only get worse. Here are some ways to ease depression.

1. Talk about your depression. If at all possible, find a trusted friend or relative and talk about the way depression is affecting your life.
2. Make a list. Think about some ways depression is affecting your life. Begin to plan ways to actively deal with it.
3. Use physical exercise to generate the body's natural healing process. Feeling better physically makes a person feel better mentally and emotionally.
4. Pamper yourself. When people are mourning, it is easy for them to neglect themselves, which only adds to their depressed state. Do something nice for yourself today.
5. Listen to your internal dialogue. Negative internal dialogue feeds depression. Listen to the way you are talking to yourself. One way to do this is to change "Why" statements to "How" statements.
6. Find a creative outlet for yourself, such as singing, playing a musical instrument, or writing poetry. Even

painting the kitchen walls or putting pictures in an album can ease depression. The idea is to choose something that you can look at or feel good about.

7. Pray. Most importantly, use prayer as a key to open doors. Pray for insight into the best ways to ease your personal type of depression. Pray for the motivation to begin. Pray to have the energy to complete your chosen task. Pray for a special friend who will stand by your side and help you fight the battle against depression. Write down your prayer requests right now.

Taking Care of Yourself

How is your health? Have you taken the time to seek medical help where necessary? Are you eating properly? How is your weight? Are you neglecting yourself on the premise that you feel poorly because you are grieving?

1. Take the time right now to write an assessment of your physical condition. Are you experiencing any of the following?

Insomnia	Fatigue
An eating disorder	A lack of energy
Constant crying	Chest pains
Shortness of breath	Nausea
Diarrhea	Memory loss
Anxiety	Headaches
Nightmares	Cold sweats
Overeating	Irregular heartbeats
Constipation	Dry mouth
Hair loss	

Any of these symptoms can be from grief. However, it is important to seek medical care to rule out any legitimate health problems.

Good Nutrition

Eating problems can either begin during the grief process or become more pronounced. Good nutrition is especially important when you are mourning. Grievers must keep their bodies in good condition so they can be strong enough to deal with their grief.

1. Write down all the food you eat in a twenty-four-hour period. Has your diet been nutritious and adequate?
2. What changes do you need to make?

Good Sleep Habits

Problems with sleep patterns may appear. Guard your sleep time carefully and take time to wind down at night before getting into bed. Use the old tried-and-true techniques of warm milk, soft music, or reading quietly before trying to fall asleep.

1. Record your sleep habits. Do you need to change any of them?
2. List a few things you might enjoy doing at the end of your day to help you wind down and prepare for sleep.

Moving Forward

God sends rainbows as a symbol of his promise to never again destroy all humanity with a flood. There is something about that splash of color appearing in the sky that should bring smiles to our faces and hope to our souls.

Are you looking around hopefully or are you bound and determined not to see anything beautiful on the horizon?

1. Stop and look around you. Take the time today to search the skies and to search your life for a touch of beauty. Right now, go to a window and look outside. What do you see? Is the sun shining and adding a golden glow to everything, or is it night with sprinkles of stars like glitter in the black velvet sky? Even a cloudy sky has character and beauty. Look at the rain or snow coming down and enjoy it.
2. Write down just one beautiful aspect of nature and think about it.

Experience the Loss

Grievers do not have to simply wait for the passage of time or allow the phases of grief to control them. They can perform tasks and take action, such as attending a grief support group or doing these exercises. By using this approach, grievers have more leverage and control of their future and can actively participate in moving forward. Grief does not go away by itself. Start right now to understand this and let yourself *experience* your loss.

1. Are you experiencing your loss in healthy ways? How? If not, write down any items that need to be changed and your plan for changing them.
2. Are there friends who could help in these areas?

Adapt to the Loss

As you experience your loss, you will be expected to adapt to your new environment. Adapting can have a wide range of meaning. You may need to assume new roles, and you may have a drastic change in your financial status; you may have become a single parent or be living alone for the first time in your life.

1. Think about ways your environment has changed. What adjustments have been necessary? These may be obvious changes or subtle ones.
2. What can you do to make the adjustment easier?
3. Is there anything you need to learn how to do? If so, write it in your workbook. Then write down the name of anyone who may be able to help with a particular need.

Along with the adjustments you will probably have assumed some new roles.

1. List your new roles.
2. Do you need to call upon friends or professionals in the weakest areas? If so, write down some possibilities.
3. Give yourself a grade on how you have done so far and set some goals for the future.

Evaluate Your Support System

Without a proper foundation, a house could not stand. The first strong wind would shake the house and blow it down. Remember the three little pigs? We, too, need to build our houses with sturdy brick.

Your loss has just shaken you to the basement level. Having a strong support system will make your future easier. Think about the people who have been supportive in the past and begin to expand your base of support.

1. Do you need to begin now to make changes to overlap the support that has disappeared with the loss of your

loved one? Do you need to add more bricks to your
house to make it sturdier?
2. Compare your past support system with your current
one.
3. What changes or additions does it need?

Reinvest Your Energy

After you have completed the previous steps, you will be
ready to reinvest your energy. This is one of the last steps
along the journey of grief.

1. Are you ready to reinvest your energy elsewhere? If not,
   what sounds interesting when you finally *do* reach that
   point? Think and pray about what you want your life
   to be like a year from now.
2. Check your local newspaper for suggestions of activities in your community and organizations that are des-
   perate for help. Think about what would be beneficial
   to you at this time or what might interest you in the
   future.
3. Set a few small goals and write them down.

Embrace the Legacy of Your Loved One

Acceptance is the last step on the road of grief. People
reach this place at different time periods, often so gradually
that sometimes they do not even recognize it. Prior to this
time, to think ahead to the rest of your life would have been
overwhelming and unnecessary, but now you will feel ready
to move forward.

An old adage asks, "How do you eat an elephant?" The
answer is, "One bite at a time." By the time you get to this
last section of exercises, you will probably have only a small
portion of the elephant left. How can you finish it off? By let-

ting the good memories gradually replace your pain and by remembering the legacy your loved one left behind.

Every person has special qualities. We remember and treasure these qualities after they die; these are the legacy they leave behind.

1. Record any legacy your loved one left you. How can you grab onto that special legacy and incorporate it into your own life?
2. Is there a way you can improve your life and the lives of others as a result of knowing your loved one? Write down the details.
3. Write a letter of thanks to your loved one for the good things he or she brought to your life.

The loss of a loved one can make you better or bitter. Stop right now and pray that you will use your loss in a productive way in the future. Let happy memories replace sad ones. Actor Paul Michael Glaser, whose wife and son died from AIDS, wrote, "The important part of the journey is to know we are not victims. There is an opportunity to learn here."

As you travel down your own journey toward healing, use any legacies you have received, along with necessary tools to make your path less bumpy. Take the time to remove roadblocks, such as anger and guilt, and try not to trip over the rocky spots brought about from depression. Nurture yourself so that you are strong and healthy, and the path will seem less difficult.

Stop often to look over your shoulder at the progress you have made and the distance you have come and then proceed forward slowly and with care.

When you reach the end of your journey of grief, allow God to continue to be your guide. May your path lead you into glorious rays of sunshine.

Notes

Chapter One: The Wound

1. Fay Angus, *How to Do Everything Right and Live to Regret It* (New York: Harper & Row, 1983), 143.
2. J. Grant Swank Jr., "The bright side of pain," *Psychology for Living,* February 1986, 20.
3. C. S. Lewis, *A Grief Observed* (New York: Seabury Press, 1963), 61–62.

Chapter Two: The Flood

1. Harold S. Kushner, *When Bad Things Happen to Good People* (New York: Schocken Books, 1981), 63.

Chapter Three: The Rainbow

1. Erich Lindemann, "Symptomatology and management of acute grief," *American Journal of Psychiatry* (1944): 101.
2. Kathleen Keating, *Hug Therapy* (Tucson: CompCare Publications, 1983), 1.
3. Angus, *How to Do Everything Right,* 160.
4. Ibid., 158.

For Further Reading

Carr, G. Lloyd, and Gwendolyn C. Carr. *The Fierce Goodbye.* Downers Grove, Ill: InterVarsity Press, 1990.
Excellent information for dealing with sudden or violent deaths.

Cowman, L.B. *Streams in the Desert.* Grand Rapids, Mich: Zondervan, 1997.
A daily devotional that speaks to the heart of the hurting with words and Scriptures that bring comfort.

Diets, Bob. *Life After Loss.* Tucson: Fisher Books, 1988.
Practical steps to take for working through the grief process.

Doka, Kenneth J., Ph.D. *Living with Grief after Sudden Loss.* Philadelphia: Taylor and Francis, 1996.
Help when the death occurred suddenly and unexpectedly, including homicide.

Ginsburg, Genevieve Davis. *Widow to Widow.* Tucson: Fisher Books, 1999.
Answers questions that widows have from her own experience.

Lord, Janice Harris. *No Time for Goodbyes.* Ventura, Calif: Pathfinder Publishing, 1987.

Help for coping with a sudden, tragic death.

Mitsch, Raymond R., and Lynn Brookside. *Grieving the Loss of Someone You Love.* Ann Arbor, Mich: Servant Publications, 1993.

Daily meditations to help you through the grieving process.

O'Connor, Nancy, Ph.D. *Letting Go with Love.* Tucson: La Mariposa Press, 1994.

Thorough explanation of the grief process. Some good advice for caregivers also.

Robinson, Rita. *Survivors of Suicide.* IBS Press, 1989.

Information to assist in accepting death from suicide.

Sittser, Gerald L. *A Grace Disguised.* Grand Rapids, Mich: Zondervan, 1998.

Deals with responding to loss as an opportunity to grow and achieve simple blessings.

Welshons, John E. *Awakening from Grief: Finding the Road Back to Joy.* Open Heart Publications, 1999.

Offers comfort with heartwarming stories.

Wolfelt, A.D. *Understanding Grief: Helping Yourself Heal.* Bristol, Penn: Accelerated Development, Inc., 1992.

Discusses the healing needs of survivors.

Wylie, Betty Jane. *Survival Guide for Widows.* New York: HarperCollins, 1984.

Practical information for women living alone. Includes information on finances, emotions, children, and spirituality.

Ziglar, Zig. *Confessions of a Grieving Christian.* Nashville: Thomas Nelson, 2000.

A best-selling author shares his personal story of loss, grief, and renewal.

Zonnebelt-Smeenge, Susan J., and Robert C. DeVries. *Getting to the Other Side of Grief: Overcoming the Loss of a Spouse.* Grand Rapids, Mich: Baker Book House, 1999.

800,000 people lose a spouse every year. This is a book especially for them.

Children

Cohen, Miriam. *Jim's Dog Muffins.* New York: Bantam, Doubleday Dell, 1984.

Subtle but good in explaining to children natural reactions to loss.

Grollman, Earl. *Explaining Death to Children.* Boston: Beacon Press, 1965.

An easy-to-read, well-written book to help understand how grief affects children.

Huntly, Theresa. *Helping Children Grieve.* Minneapolis: Augsburg Press, 1991.

To help the reader answer children's questions and guide them in coping with their feelings.

Mellonie, Bryan, and Robert Ingpen. *Lifetimes.* New York: Bantam, 1983.

A colorful storybook to read to young children.

Schaefer, Dan, and Christine Lyons. *How Do We Tell the Children?* New York: Newmarket Press, 1986.

Everything a person needs to know about dealing with children of all ages and death. Special crisis section for quick reference.

Slatery, Kathryn. *Grandma I'll Miss You.* Colorado Springs: David C. Cook, 1993.

A good way to introduce children to the subject of death.

June Cerza Kolf spent fifteen years as a hospice volunteer coordinator for home health care agencies in California. During that time she led grief support groups and did bereavement follow-up visits along with being a hospice volunteer. She is the author of *How Can I Help?* and *Comfort and Care in a Final Illness.* Her inspirational work appears in a wide variety of books and magazines, including the Chicken Soup books, *The Christian Reader, Guideposts,* and *Mature Living.* She has published over fifty articles on grief.

Comfort, answers, and hope for suicide survivors

The trauma of losing a loved one to suicide is so devastating for survivors that the typical coping mechanisms no longer work for them. For this reason, they need specific guidance to help them function and heal.

With deep sensitivity, June Cerza Kolf leads readers through mourning to acceptance in *Standing in the Shadow*. This brief, to-the-point book helps suicide survivors realize the tragedy was out of their control, release their guilt and anger, and gain the power of prayer. It covers the heart of thirty-four topics and questions on suicide, including depression, forgiveness, and the salvation of those who commit suicide.

STANDING IN THE
SHADOW
Help and Encouragement for Suicide Survivors

June Cerza Kolf

Standing in the Shadow
*Help and Encouragement
for Suicide Survivors*
ISBN 0-8010-6395-7
Paperback
80 pages